BRITAIN IN PICTURES

THE BRITISH PEOPLE IN PICTURES

ENGLISH
HYMNS AND HYMN WRITERS

GENERAL EDITOR
W. J. TURNER

The Editor is most grateful to all those who have
so kindly helped in the selection of illustrations
especially to officials of the various public
Museums Libraries and Galleries and
to all others who have generously
allowed pictures and MSS
to be reproduced

ENGLISH HYMNS AND HYMN WRITERS

ADAM FOX

WITH
8 PLATES IN COLOUR
AND
22 ILLUSTRATIONS IN
BLACK & WHITE

COLLINS · 14 ST. JAMES'S PLACE · LONDON
MCMXLVII

PRODUCED BY
ADPRINT LIMITED LONDON

PRINTED IN GREAT BRITAIN
BY JARROLD AND SONS LTD NORWICH
ON MELLOTEX BOOK PAPER MADE
BY TULLIS RUSSELL AND CO LTD MARKINCH SCOTLAND

LIST OF ILLUSTRATIONS

PLATES IN COLOUR

BLACK AND WHITE ILLUSTRATIONS

This is the day when Christ arose
So early from the dead
Woodcut from Watts's *Divine and Moral Songs for Children*

HYMNS A NATIONAL INSTITUTION

IT takes no long argument to prove that Hymn Singing is a national institution in Great Britain. It is so rather in the same way as cricket. On Saturday afternoons in the summer a great many of our countrymen will be engaged in a game of cricket, and whether it be at the county ground or on the village green cricket always has its spectators. And on the next day, and in fact on Sundays all the year round, a much larger number will go to church or chapel, and almost all of them, when they get there, will sing a hymn or two, whatever else divine service provides for them. And this hymn singing has settled down, like cricket, into a particular form. It consists in singing to a simple tune several stanzas of not at all elaborate English rhymed verse. The stanzas usually have four or eight lines, less frequently six. The commonest form of stanza is the same as that of the old ballads. It has alternate lines of eight and six syllables, and the short lines rhyme with each other. Sometimes the eight-syllabled lines rhyme with each other too. As the lines of each stanza correspond in length and accent, each may be sung to the same tune. The tune is usually harmonised in four parts, but most of the singers do not attempt the underparts; they sing the air. The words are in a book of which they nearly all have a copy. In some of the most popular hymns there is a refrain or chorus. The singing is usually accompanied on an organ, or if there is no organ, then on a piano. The harmonium, though sometimes used for the purpose, cannot be recommended, and is falling into disuse.

This way of singing hymns seems so very ordinary as hardly to merit description, but actually it was only arrived at after a great deal of experiment, a good deal of which turned out to be misconceived. It was only in the eighteenth century that hymn singing in the modern manner came in, but once it was hit upon it soon established itself as a national, and at times an almost universal, custom. Of course a great many of our national customs are a great deal older than the eighteenth century. But the reason why hymn singing has been comparatively speaking a latecomer is really quite obvious. It is that congregational hymn singing, as we call it, requires hymn books, and it was not possible till the art of printing got well under way to produce hymn books numerous enough or cheap enough for this purpose. In fact it was only at the end of the seventeenth century that such a project became practicable.

EARLY CHRISTIAN HYMNS

THIS does not mean, however, that there were no hymns before printing. On the contrary, the Christian Church has always sung hymns. The New Testament tells us that on the night before the Crucifixion Jesus and the Apostles sang a hymn (Mark xiv. 26), possibly Psalm 118. There are even a few fragments of hymn words to be found in St. Paul's Epistles.

> Awake thou that sleepest, and arise from the dead, and Christ shall give thee light (Ephesians v. 14)

appears to be such a fragment, and a metrical one is in 1 Timothy iii. 16:

> God was manifest in the flesh, justified in the Spirit, seen of angels, preached unto the Gentiles, believed on in the world, received up into glory.

In the earliest account of a Christian service from a pagan pen the younger Pliny tells us that the Christians on the southern shores of the Black Sea were accustomed to sing a hymn to Christ at daybreak on Sundays "in turn" (*invicem*), that is to say antiphonally, as we now usually sing the Psalms. This was about A.D. 110. The subsequent development of Christian Church music is obscure, and to attempt to trace it would in any

CIII· IPSI DAVI O·

BENEDICANIMA mea dno: dne ds meus magnificatus es uehementer: Confessionem &decorem induisti: amictus lumine sicut uestimento ; Extendens caelum sicut pellem : quitegis aquis superiora eius Quipones nubem ascensum

tuum: quiambulas super pennas uentorum Quifacis angelos tuos spc &ministros tuos ignem urentem Quifundasti terram super stabilitatem suam noninch nabitur insclm saeculi ; Abyssus sicut uestimentu Amictus eius sup montes

stabunt aquae ; A bincrepatione tua fugi ent auoce tonitrui tui formidabunt Ascendunt montes &de scendunt campi: inlocu quem fundasti eis ; erminum posuisti quenon transgredientur neq con uertentur operire terra

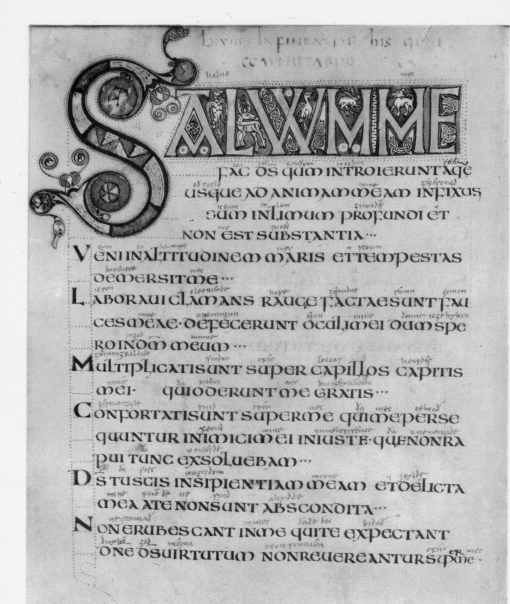

A PAGE FROM THE EARLIEST ENGLISH PSALTER
MS. containing St. Jerome's Roman Version
with Canticles and Hymns written in England in the 8th century
The Anglo-Saxon interlinear translation was added in the 9th century

case not be relevant here. But we do know that when the great Arian controversy vexed the Church in the third century, the Arian heretics composed verses which could be fitted to the tunes of the day and sang them by way of propagating their views. The orthodox replied with rival songs, and such singing presently found its place in the Church at large. To seek inspiration from folk-songs for hymn tunes like this has been of common occurrence ever since, and our newest hymn books to-day owe much to it. Of the early hymn writers Prudentius (about A.D. 400) is the best known. He is the author of a number of Latin hymns of which *Earth has many a noble city* is a good one in an English dress. Adam of St. Victor (about A.D. 1150) is perhaps the greatest of all Latin hymn writers.

It is impossible to consider hymns from the historical or artistic point of view without taking into account the old Latin hymns, for they have in a high degree some of the qualities which great hymns ought to possess. The Latin language is so admirably suited to the purpose. It has a natural solemnity which makes it possible to say what is obvious or familiar so that it seems important. It sounds important too. And that is very useful in a hymn where there is no opportunity of dwelling on the meaning while you sing, and therefore no time to puzzle out a deep thought or admire an unusual one. What the hymn says must at least seem familiar, but unfortunately the familiar breeds contempt and is in danger of seeming uninteresting. But Latin makes ordinary things interesting. The great truths and commonplaces keep alive in Latin and that is just what is wanted. It is not surprising that many of our most famous English hymns are translated from the Latin. And it is worth a digression to say that in fitting their words to the popular tunes the Latin-speaking Christians neglected the strict quantities of Latin versification and scanned their lines much more loosely by stress, as we do in English to-day. But in return for this relaxation they introduced the beautiful device of rhyme which was quite unknown in the old classical poetry. This gift of rhyme, valuable not only to hymns but to all poetry, we owe to the Christians of the fourth century.

It is obvious, however, when we think of it, that the use of hymns in those days and for many a long year to come could not be the same as their use to-day. The words, not to speak of the music, had to be copied by hand, and although it is surprising to find how much writing was done in a scriptorium or writing house, whether commercial or monastic, and how moderate the price of manuscripts was, yet they could not be cheap in the way we were thinking of just now. And in fact though many hymns were accumulated through the centuries, they were mainly sung on special occasions or in their own particular place. They occupied roughly the same place in the Church as national songs or school songs do now. *God Save the King* is customarily heard on certain occasions, and people join

9

in and sing whatever they know of the words. In recent years Blake's "Jerusalem" (*And did those feet*) and Arkwright's *O valiant hearts* have often been sung in places where it was expected that the words would be known by many. And this is always so at school when the School Song is sung. These are all genuine hymns in the old sense. The tune has been learnt by ear and the words by heart, though some copies of both must be in circulation from time to time.

So it was in the Church before printing became common. The special hymns which in different parts of Christendom were sung at Christmas or Easter became widely diffused and were largely common property. Others belonged to particular cathedrals and were often in honour of local saints or sung on particular occasions or at particular services. They had the same kind of history as folk-songs and the same place in the affections of the people. Over a period of many centuries a great number of hymns were accumulated and were from time to time collected into hymnaries by some diligent monk. But this was not by way of making a hymn book in the modern sense. No church would have a great repertory of hymns, and very often when a hymn was sung, the choir gathered round one great book to sing it while the people listened. And some of the pieces in the hymnaries were not so much hymns as sacred lyrics intended for private reading and personal devotion.

EARLY ENGLISH HYMNS

WHILE therefore it would be untrue to say that the introduction of printing gave rise to hymn singing, it certainly did enormously increase its scope. What may be said is that whereas, before printing made books numerous, people at church looked forward to the familiar and fixed parts of the service, as soon as they could have a book in their hands, whether it was a Bible or a prayer book or a hymn book, they began to look forward most to the variable parts and especially to the parts where they could sing popular tunes and easily come by the full and correct version of the words. And in Britain hymn singing assumed a particular importance for two reasons; first, because the Reformation here was particularly directed towards giving the people a part and an interest in the services they attended by simplifying them and having them in English, and secondly because the English are very fond of poetry and not very ambitious in music. Poetry is the great national art, and it comes easily to almost all of us to find pleasure in verse and rhyme. Music means less to us, but what we mostly care for in it is a kind of charm and cheerfulness which find their best expression in Church singing or something of the sort. In Wales very notably singing of a high order seems to be within

BEATUS PAGE: INITIAL OF PSALM 1
From a thirteenth-century Psalter executed at Peterborough

the reach of almost all, and in England it might be so, and perhaps soon
will be. For in the last forty years the English have apparently made up
their minds that they are musical.

Of early English hymnody not a great deal remains. But a number of
carols and some religious instructions in verse show the great simplicity
and tenderness of old English before it became literary and called in Latin
to aid in the expression of more complicated thoughts. In practice, in fact,
we often describe a piece as a carol rather than a hymn just because Latin

11

words and feeling are absent from it. *The Oxford Book of Carols* contains quite a lot of this material with interesting notes, and most of the anthologies of English Verse which begin at the beginning have some of these pieces to show. *I sing of a maiden that is makeless* (matchless) is now often heard, also the *Coventry Carol* from the Pageant of the Shear-men and Tailors, *Lully, lulla, thou little tiny child*, which in the pageant precedes the entry of King Herod:

> Herod, the king
> In his raging
> Charged he hath this day
> His men of might,
> In his own sight,
> All young children to slay.

The tone of these fifteenth-century poems was lost in course of time, and has only been caught again at happy moments, as in Christina Rossetti's deeply affecting *In the bleak mid-winter*:

> Angels and Archangels
> May have gathered there,
> Cherubim and Seraphim
> Thronged the air:
> But only his mother
> In her maiden bliss
> Worshipped the Beloved
> With a kiss.

THE METRICAL PSALMS

WE pass on and come to the age of the Tudors. What is commonly said of this period would make one expect that hymns would come out of it. It seems to have been a great time for music. You get the impression that everyone of high degree sang and touched the lute. But the tendencies of the time worked both for and against the introduction of hymns: the Reformation made a way for them, but it also stood in their way. How this might be is well seen in the case of Merbecke, who was condemned to death in some political upheaval and specially reprieved by Henry VIII in order to set to music the sung portions of the services in the new English prayer book which was then in the making. He accomplished the work to perfection, but it had no success at the time nor at all until about a hundred years ago. And why?

12

STERNHOLD AND HOPKINS'S *WHOLE BOOKE OF PSALMES*,
Imprint of the first edition 1562

Apparently because Merbecke turned Calvinist and as such he disapproved
of music in church. He put his own great work out of circulation.
Similarly Puritanism was on the whole an obstacle to hymn singing for a
long time. One hears of psalm-singing, not of hymn-singing Puritans, and
that was because the strong feeling for the Bible made many think
it profane to use anything from other sources in divine service. The
result was that the use of sacred verse in church was limited for a very
long time to metrical versions of the Psalms. These prevented hymns
being sung, but they also created a tradition upon which hymn singing
eventually based itself. The story of the metrical Psalter therefore needs
to be noticed here.

But it is a very complicated and disorderly story. In the end the whole
Psalter came to be versified in France and in England and in Scotland,

13

but the form it took and the tunes that got attached to it seem almost matters of chance, and there was the same confused borrowing of words and music that there is between the different hymn books to-day. The first notable stage in the progress of the work occurs perhaps in 1562. In that year the Psalter in French became available in a complete form at Geneva. Some of the original translations had been by a great French poet, Marot (1497–1544), and a real genius called Louis Bourgeois composed numerous tunes to supplement the existing stock. The metres were various and sometimes elaborate, and the tunes were noble. In the same year the complete Psalter also appeared in England, the so-called "Old Version," edited by Sternhold and Hopkins. Not many true poets, perhaps none, contributed to the work, and in the course of its completion the tunes got fewer and fewer. The idea of a different tune for each Psalm was completely abandoned. Borrowings were made from Bourgeois, but he fared badly because his tunes, written for the elegant French verse, had to be forcibly fitted to the cruder English metres, and they suffered in the process. In the end almost all of Sternhold and Hopkins's words went out of use and much too much of Bourgeois too, though the "Old Hundredth" is his, and is still attached to *All people that on earth do dwell* which is the metrical version of Psalm 100.

It so happened that Sternhold and Hopkins had borrowed many of the later Psalms from a Genevan Psalter in English by William Kethe which had appeared in 1561. This contained eighty-seven psalms and they were destined to have a long life because they were taken over (with forty-two from Sternhold and Hopkins and twenty-one new ones) to form the complete metrical Psalter of the Scottish Presbyterians. In Scotland they are still in regular use. Very characteristic and famous in this book is the version of Psalm 124 by Whittingham, set to one of Bourgeois's tunes. Dr. Alan Don of St. Margaret's, Westminster, now Dean of Westminster, chose it for the Thanksgiving Service on May 8th 1945, when the House of Commons attended in state. Many of the Members, including the Prime Minister, Mr. Churchill, were said to have been much struck by it.

> Now Israel may say, and that truly,
> If that the Lord had not our cause maintain'd;
> If that the Lord had not our right sustain'd,
> When cruel men against us furiously
> Rose up in wrath, to make of us their prey;
>
> Then certainly they had devour'd us all,
> And swallow'd quick, for ought that we could deem;
> Such was their rage, as we might well esteem.
> And as fierce floods before them all things drown,
> So had they brought our soul to death quite down.

THAT THE LORDS HOVSE SHOVLD BE BVILT. 3 THEN CAME THE WORD OF THE LORD BY HAGGAI THE PROPHETT SAYNG 4 IS IT TYME FOR YOVRSELVES (O YEE) TO DWELL IN YOVR SEILED HOVSES & THIS HOVSE LYE WASTE

HAGGAI CHAP:ii:VER2 THVS SPEAKETH THE LORD OF HOSTS THIS PEOPLE SAIE, THE TYME IS NOT YET COME.

IT IS WRITTEN: MY HOVSE IS THE HOVSE OF PRAYER: &c;

PREACHING AT ST. PAUL'S CROSS IN THE SEVENTEENTH CENTURY
Engraving from Wilkinson's *Londina Illustrata*

There is grandeur in this, though it must be allowed that many of the
pieces in all the older versions are rough and clumsy. To versify the
Psalms adequately is in truth hideously difficult. There were always plenty
of people who were dissatisfied with Sternhold and Hopkins, and tried
their hand at improving upon them. Archbishop Parker published a
version of the whole Psalter about 1567 with some of the tunes by Tallis.
George Sandys did the like with twenty-four new tunes by Henry Lawes

15

in 1638, but neither of these was meant for congregational use. The names of Day, Playford, and Ravenscroft deserve to be recalled for their efforts to improve the music.

At the end of the seventeenth century the general dissatisfaction came to a head, and an attempt was made to allay it by the publication in 1696 of a new version—the New Version of Tate and Brady. Tate was Poet Laureate, and the dedication of the work to the King gave it a sort of official sanction. The Old and the New Versions contended for acceptance for a very long time just as the Authorised and Revised Versions of the Bible do now. Actually both were in use when the singing of metrical psalms finally expired in the English Church. The New Version suited the taste of the age of Anne. It is smoother and less contorted than the Old Version. Yet in many places it is perforce more ingenious than graceful. *One day in thy courts is better than a thousand* is put into verse and incidentally made clearer by the following lines, but it is scarcely improved:

> For in thy courts one single day
> 'Tis better to attend
> Than, Lord, in any place besides
> A thousand days to spend.

This is from Tate and Brady's version of Psalm 84. But they could do better. Their Psalm 42, *As pants the hart*, is a popular hymn. So is Psalm 34, *Through all the changing scenes of life*. For the most part they kept to the Ballad Metre, which in consequence came to be called C.M. or Common Measure. The people knew it, and could manage it best when they came to sing in church.

This singing of the Metrical Psalter was a good preparation for hymn singing, but it also had a more direct part in introducing actual hymns into the English Church. In addition to the Psalms the Old Version of 1562 had the Te Deum, Nunc Dimittis, the Athanasian Creed, the Lord's Prayer, and the Ten Commandments in metre, and also eight hymns. Tate and Brady had a similar supplement which included *While shepherds watched their flocks by night*. Eight years before that a small collection of hymns to supplement the Psalms had been made for use in the parishes of St. Martin in the Fields and St. James's, Piccadilly. In the first year of the eighteenth century Playford's *Psalms and Hymns* of 1671 was enlarged and contained twelve hymns, and in 1709 enlarged again to seventeen hymns with new tunes by various composers, including William Croft and Jeremiah Clark. So the gates were slowly opened to admit the flood. The voices that claimed that only paraphrases from the Bible should be used in church grew fainter, and hymns much in our modern manner began to appear in abundance. Isaac Watts (1674–1748) may be called the first modern hymn writer.

COMING FROM EVENING CHURCH, SHOREHAM, KENT
Tempera painting by Samuel Palmer, 1830
By courtesy of the Trustees of the Tate Gallery

SONGS,

DIVINE AND MORAL,

FOR

THE USE OF CHILDREN.

BY THE

REV. ISAAC WATTS, D.D.

LONDON :

CHARLES TILT, 86, FLEET STREET.

M DCCC XXXII.

The Tulip and the Butterfly
Appear in gayer Coats than I
Woodcut from Dr. Watts's *Hymns for Children*
Coloured by John Constable for his daughter Emily, 1844
By courtesy of the Director of the Victoria & Albert Museum

THE SEVENTEENTH CENTURY

IT would be a mistake, however, to suppose that in the seventeenth century there was no contribution to hymnody except the supplements to the Metrical Psalters. A great many short religious poems were written and intended to be sung to the accompaniment of some sort of musical instrument, and among their authors some of the most famous names in English literature are to be found—Milton, Donne, George Herbert, Vaughan, for example. But most of these poems might be described as hymnoid rather than actual hymns. Many of them are in the very first rank as lyrical poetry. Such are Milton's "Hymn on the Morning of Christ's Nativity" (*It was the winter wild*), Donne's "Hymn to God the Father" (*Wilt thou forgive that sin where I begun*), Herbert's "Easter" (*Rise heart: thy Lord is risen*), Vaughan's "Peace" (*My soul, there is a country*). And these and others like them have in our own time had music composed for them and are sung in church. But they were not written for that purpose. They were intended for personal and private use. It is a fairly safe conjecture that they will not find a permanent place in our hymn books. They are too elaborate in thought and often in structure. They are more the stuff of which anthems are made. Only the simpler pieces will survive, less masterly as literature, but more manageable as hymns. Of this kind are Milton's *Let us with a gladsome mind*, Herbert's *Let all the world in every corner sing*, and Bishop Ken's Morning and Evening Hymns, *Awake my soul and with the sun*, and *Glory to Thee, my God, this night*.

One very prolific writer of the period really intended something like a hymn book, and he was a good poet too. This is George Wither (1588–1667), the author of *Hymnes and Songs of the Church* (1623). But he did not go about it in the right way, and very little of his verse has survived in the hymn books of to-day, though *Songs of Praise* contains three pieces which have not as yet any vogue. But Wither made a great contribution indirectly, for he got Orlando Gibbons to write sixteen tunes for his book. After a long oblivion these are now finding a place everywhere. The best known is perhaps the little air which has got itself attached to Sir H. W. Baker's *Jesu, grant me this, I pray*.

Two other seventeenth-century names should by no means be omitted. John Bunyan (1628–1688) has given us the very popular *He who would valiant be*, and Richard Baxter (1615–1691) wrote *Lord, it belongs not to my care* and *He wants not friends that hath Thy love*. John Cosin (1594–1672), afterwards Bishop of Durham, is notable in a particular way. He composed a book of devotion into which he put some of the ancient office hymns of the medieval church. The book was called *A Collection of Private Devotions in the Practice of the Ancient Church called the Hours of Prayer*, 1627. From it the hymn *Come, Holy Ghost, our souls inspire*, was taken into the Book of Common Prayer. But Cosin was before his time. The Office Hymns were not introduced into *public* worship or sung in church till the last hundred years, and many of them not before the present century.

This seventeenth century was a time of experiment, and by the beginning of the eighteenth century the experiments were over, and what was required of a hymn writer had become clear. The old solid versification and tune-making of the Metrical Psalters was the pattern, but the art needed to be liberated in its application to new material. The eighteenth century affected this liberation, and made hymn writing and hymn singing in Britain what they are. In this matter, as in so many matters, it was the great age.

ISAAC WATTS, 1674–1748

THERE are three great names among the hymn writers of the eighteenth century, Isaac Watts, Charles Wesley, and William Cowper. Of these, Watts is perhaps the most important, Wesley the most successful, and Cowper the most famous. I call Watts the most important because he brought several new ideas of importance into hymn writing. He was the first person to produce a successful hymn book in the modern sense. It is called *Hymns and Spiritual Songs in Three Books*. It came out in 1707. The First Book contains 150 pieces which he describes as "Collected from the Scriptures." Here he has paraphrased passages of Scripture much in the style of Tate and Brady except that he happened to be a much better poet. But in the Second Book he launched out, and it contains 170 pieces "Compos'd on Divine Subjects." These are the sort of pieces we now think of as hymns. The Third Book contained pieces for the Lord's Supper. The whole work is written in the simplest metres so as to fit tunes which are suitable for congregational singing. The book is provided with an Index of First Lines, and another of Titles and Contents. In comparison with anything that went before it, it is a very practical book; it had a large circulation from the start. And no wonder, for it was not only the first hymn book that had in view the actual demand, but it was an extremely good one. Watts, though a strict Calvinist, was a cheerful, singing soul, a severe person but with something of a twinkle. He was also an admirable versifier. On every page of his poetic works you find good things. Look at such a work as *The Oxford Dictionary of Quotations* under his name, and there are a surprising number of well-known lines, and some admirable bits of poetry.

His hymns have to a large extent been gradually excluded from the books owing to their now obsolete theology, but where this objection is

A CHURCH SERVICE
Engraving by C. Bowles, *c.* 1700

not present, they are at times brilliantly successful. They are so moving, so relevant, so tidy, and they fit the simple tunes of his time so easily and well. The most celebrated of them is *O God, our help in ages past*, in which the solid virtues of both words and tune have combined to make a hymn almost indispensable on national occasions. But there are others too which show no signs of growing old. *Jesus shall reign where'er the sun* and *Give us the wings of faith to rise* and *How bright those glorious spirits shine* are sung everywhere because they are so cheerful, and Watts can beautify graver thoughts too, as in *There is a land of pure delight*:

> Sweet fields beyond the swelling flood
>   Stand dress'd in living green;
> So to the Jews old Canaan stood,
>   While Jordan roll'd between.
>
> But timorous mortals start and shrink
>   To cross the narrow sea,
> And linger shivering on the brink,
>   And fear to launch away.
>
> Oh, could we make our doubts remove,
>   Those gloomy doubts that rise,
> And see the Canaan that we love
>   With unbeclouded eyes:
>
> Could we but climb where Moses stood,
>   And view the landscape o'er;
> Not Jordan's stream, nor death's cold flood,
>   Should fright us from the shore.

This is admirably scriptural, but it is admirable poetry too. And Watts ought not to be neglected by those who admire poetry, even though they do not care for hymns.

He was a pioneer in a special way when as a sort of supplement to his hymns he produced a modest little book of about forty pieces entitled *Divine Songs attempted in Easy Language for the use of Children*. This was a novel attempt indeed, but one which has amply justified itself. Most hymn books now have a section "For the Young" or "At Catechism." The children Watts had in mind would perhaps seem rather old-fashioned to us, at any rate the Divine Songs appear rather old-fashioned and are not in use to-day. But *Let dogs delight to bark and bite* (XVI) and *How doth the little busy bee* (XX) were still

Now's the time for mirth and play,
Saturday's an holiday
From *Hymns for the Amusement of*
Children, 1772

household sayings not so very long ago. The writing is often very neat, of which just one example must suffice:

> How proud we are! how fond to shew
> Our clothes, and call them rich and new!
> When the poor sheep and silk-worm wore
> That very clothing long before.

Watts had something more than a Children's Service in view. In his preface, addressed "to all that are concerned in the Education of Children," he supposes that being in verse the songs will be learnt by heart, and "this," he says, "will be a constant furniture for the minds of children, that they may have something to think upon when alone, and sing over to themselves. This may sometimes give their thoughts a divine turn, and raise a young meditation." A rather sweet picture of a child alone!

He must have been a delightful man. He was most of his life minister of an Independent chapel, and for thirty-five years he lived with Sir Thomas and Lady Abney at Stoke Newington.

He there enjoyed the amenities of a fine house and garden and plenty of fresh air, which meant much to him, for his health was delicate. His congregation provided him with an assistant who ministered to them when he was not well enough himself. He was thus able to come by a good deal of leisure to write his hymns as well as a successful logic and other educational and theological works.

His bust by Banks in Westminster Abbey shows a rather unusual face with a keenly concentrated expression.

H Y M N   XXIX.

Againſt Quarrelling and Fighting.

I.

LET dogs delight to bark and bite,
  For God has made then ſo;
Let bears and lions growl and fight,
  For 'tis their nature too.

II.

But, children, you ſhould never let
  Such angry paſſions riſe;
Your little hands were never made
To tear each other's eyes.

Woodcut from Dr. Watts's *Divine and Moral Songs for Children*

21

ALMOST alongside of this bust is a double medallion relief of John and Charles Wesley seen in profile. And this is a fitting collocation of monuments, because the Wesleys owed so much to hymns and in that connection owed so much to Watts. The work which John Wesley did was what is called a Ministry of Conversion. It was of vast extent. He spoke to an enormous number of people about turning from a careless or a wicked life to a godly and religious life, and to very many of them he spoke with success. And quite early on he saw how useful it was to set them singing hymns and what a powerful effect the hymns could have. He issued one hymn book after the other. Some of the hymns were taken from Watts, some he translated from the German himself, but far the greatest number were composed by his brother Charles. The Methodist Movement, as it was called, had been going for some thirty years, when in 1780 the various books were consolidated into *A Collection of Hymns for the use of the people called Methodists*, amounting to close on 540 hymns in all. John Wesley wrote a manly preface to the book in which he said of it: "It is not so large as to be either cumbersome or expensive: and it is large enough to contain such a variety of hymns, as will not soon be threadbare. It is large enough to contain all the important truths of our most holy religion, whether speculative or practical; yea, to illustrate them all, and to prove them both by Scripture and reason: and this is done in a regular order. The hymns are not carelessly jumbled together, but carefully ranged under proper heads, according to the experience of real Christians. So that this book is, in effect, a little body of experimental and practical divinity. As but a small part of these hymns is of my own composing, I do not think it inconsistent with modesty to declare that I am persuaded no such hymn book as this has yet been published in the English language."

He was right. No such book had been published, and every subsequent book can only be an attempt to improve upon this one, or adjust and amplify the contents for a different denominational outlook. What were "proper heads" in view of the work Wesley was doing may not for example quite suit the needs of the Church of England in the second quarter of the twentieth century. But at any rate many pieces from the Methodist collection find a place in every hymn book, and above all English hymn singing certainly owes to

ISAAC WATTS
Detail of the Bust by Banks
Westminster Abbey

John Wesley the theological element which deeply marks it, the expression of an evangelical faith reduced to simple terms. The sort of thing which Wesley meant by "proper heads" is well illustrated by the nine sections of Part IV of the book designed respectively for Believers Rejoicing, Fighting, Praying, Watching, Working, Suffering, Seeking for full Redemption, Saved, Interceding for the World. Most of these would now be once more "jumbled together" under the heading of General Hymns, but the nine kinds would still be there all right. What was almost wholly wanting in Wesley's Hymn Book was hymns for the Church's seasons, but then it was a missionary hymn book. He was not dealing

"THE BEST OF ALL IS, GOD IS WITH US."

JOHN AND CHARLES WESLEY
Medallion from the Wesley Memorial
Westminster Abbey

with people who had been going to church year in and year out. He did issue some pamphlets with hymns for particular festivals such as Christmas and Ascension Day.

Charles Wesley had written most of the pieces in the Collection of 1780, but even so they are only a fraction of his whole output. He is reckoned to have composed more than 7,000 hymns altogether. It might be thought that he probably sacrificed quality to quantity, though no doubt in such a large number there would be bound to be some good ones. But it is really impossible to depreciate him in this way. He is indisputably the greatest of English hymn writers. This may be shown quite objectively merely by mentioning his most famous hymns: *Hark! the herald-angels sing; Jesu, Lover of my soul; Let saints on earth in concert sing; Love Divine, all loves excelling; O for a thousand tongues to sing* (which is Hymn 1 in the book of 1780); *Rejoice, the Lord is King; Soldiers of Christ arise;* to which must be added most of *Lo! He comes with clouds descending.* No other writer has such a list as this to show, every one of them an admirable performance, and, what is more, very frequently sung everywhere.

Yet Wesley's skill is difficult to discover. His merits are not nearly so easy to describe as those of Watts. Their respective virtues may be tested by comparing *Let saints on earth in concert sing* with *There is a land of pure delight,* or *Rejoice, the Lord is King* with *Come, let us join our cheerful songs.* There are obvious similarities, yet there are obvious

23

differences. The sound is different, and the feeling too. Wesley has more of a lyric touch but less substance. You would think Wesley more musical than Watts, as indeed he was. It could not be said that he is happier than Watts, but his ear and heart are lighter; he is lighter built altogether, more springy and vivacious. And one quality he has most noticeably. His effect is cumulative, and he strikes a note of urgency. He tells you what is happening *now,* and very often he is telling somebody to do something.

> E'en *now* to their eternal home
> There pass some spirits blest;

or

> Finish then Thy new creation,

so he adjures the Divine Love; and in a less well known but very powerful hymn, *Hosanna in the highest,* he suddenly cries out with startling effect, "Shout, all our elder brethren." He is full of imperatives. His hymns have also gained something from the fact that he wrote so many of them, though it is true they have often had to be altered before they are quite satisfactory. But they have not too much finish. The thoughts are never far-fetched. He took what was nearest to hand provided it was good enough, with the result that we all feel he has said just what we should have liked to say ourselves, if we had the wit. He is not nearly so neat as Watts, nor has he the same range of fancy, but he presents a more universal experience of God. He has been criticised for saying the same thing over and over again. If so, he is capable of doing it with unabated force and variety.

There was a lot of music in the family. Samuel Wesley (1766–1837) was his son and Samuel Sebastian Wesley (1810–1876) was his grandson. He himself had a good voice and led the singing of his own hymns. We know what sort of singing this would be from John Wesley's express directions in the matter:

"Suit the tune to the words. Avoid complex tunes, which it is scarcely possible to sing with devotion. Repeating the same words so often, especially while another repeats different words, shocks all common sense, necessarily brings in dead formality, and has no more religion in it than a Lancashire hornpipe. Sing no anthems. Do not suffer the people to sing too slow. In every society, let them learn to sing, and let them always learn our own tunes first. Let the women constantly sing their parts alone. Let no man sing with them, unless he understands the notes, and sings the bass, as it is pricked down in the book. Introduce no new tunes till they are perfect in the old. Let no organ be placed anywhere, till proposed in the Conference. Recommend our tune-book everywhere; and if you cannot sing yourself, choose a person or two in each place to pitch the tune for you. Exhort everyone in the congregation to sing, not one in ten only."

'MY FIRST SERMON'
The Artist's Daughter in Winchelsea Church
Oil Painting by Sir John Everett Millais, 1863
By courtesy of the Librarian of the Guildhall Library

'MY SECOND SERMON'
The Artist's Daughter in Winchelsea Church
Oil painting by Sir John Everett Millais, 1864
By courtesy of the Librarian of the Guildhall Library

WILLIAM COWPER, 1731–1800

THE third great name among the eighteenth-century hymn writers is that of William Cowper, well known as a poet of great accomplishments. His health was very poor, and in consequence he lived a very retired life in Buckinghamshire, and sought relief from melancholia in the quietest country recreations. In these he found material for the most delightful letters and the most charming poetry. His chief poem, *The Task*, is a discourse on things rural and domestic, which is guided by the surest taste. Charles Lamb referred to it as Cowper's "divine chit-chat." When he digressed to the topics of the day, the poet's judgment sometimes strayed, though he is the author of the acceptable sentiment, "England, with all thy faults I love thee still."

He lived with some people called Unwin at a place called Olney. It is said that he went to stay with them for a fortnight and stopped twenty-two years. The household spent a lot of time in singing hymns and in "religious conversation," and Mrs. Unwin and his other friends were always trying to think of things for Cowper to do which would divert him from these fits of religious despair, sometimes amounting to madness, into which he fell.

He made friends with the parson of the place, the Rev. John Newton (1725–1807), and between them they started to make a hymn book. In the course of the work Cowper broke down, but he managed to contribute sixty-eight pieces. Newton's contributions were four times as many. The book is deeply evangelical and largely concerned with personal religious experiences. Much of it is not suitable for congregational use and never could have been, but some of our greatest hymns are in it. Newton himself wrote *Glorious things of Thee are spoken* and *How sweet the name of Jesus sounds* and a few others that are well known. The remarkable thing about them is that they are so literary. The language is choice, and Newton's language had not always been literary or choice. He used to call himself "the old African blasphemer" because he had been the captain of a slave ship. But in the strength of his vocation he had wonderfully overcome his want of education. He ended his long life as a much respected City Rector, the incumbent of St. Mary Woolnoth. He had a wholesome but rather overwhelming influence over Cowper.

Cowper contributed to the Olney book one of the very best-known hymns, *Hark, my soul! it is the Lord*, and also *God moves in a mysterious way*, which he composed on recovering from one of his fits of despair, in which he had meditated suicide. Another of his is *Oh! for a closer walk with God*, and in *There is a fountain filled with blood* his skill has used almost with success evangelical language now hardly admissible. Not many others by him are often sung, but they are perhaps less well known than they should be. Cowper is a very elegant writer of verse, and his religion, while

25

it lacks, and in fact rejects, Charles Wesley's happiness, surpasses him in the expression of hope and gratitude.

> Ye fearful saints, fresh courage take;
> The clouds ye so much dread
> Are big with mercy, and shall break
> In blessings on your head.
>
> Judge not the Lord by feeble sense,
> But trust Him for His grace;
> Behind a frowning providence
> He hides a smiling face.
>
> Blind unbelief is sure to err,
> And scan His work in vain;
> God is His own interpreter,
> And He will make it plain.

You cannot ask a hymn writer for more than that.

ADDISON, TOPLADY, AND OTHERS

CERTAIN writers of the eighteenth century showed themselves capable of writing as good a hymn as any, but stand rather in the background from the fewness of their pieces. Joseph Addison (1672–1719) by the tone of his Essays seems to suggest that he might be able to write a good hymn, and he showed that this was so by printing four specimens of sacred verse in *The Spectator* in 1712. Their appearance in such a fashionable periodical indicates the general interest there then was in that sort of thing among people of education and leisure. *When all thy mercies, O my God*, is in every way suitable to be sung as a hymn, though much too long in its original form. *The spacious firmament on high* is perhaps rather too fanciful for the purpose. The paraphrase of Psalm 23, *The Lord my pasture shall prepare*, reacting from the treatment of the same Psalm in the Metrical Psalters, is rather self-consciously graceful, though it is a beautiful piece of poetry. The fourth of Addison's hymns, *How are thy servants blest, O Lord*, has been sung rather fitfully. It is a genuine hymn, but falls at last into what was always Addison's danger, namely insipidity. Addison also printed in *The Spectator* a hymn by Watts, and rather later, another of his own composition. All six pieces are in the *English Hymnal*.

Then there is Philip Doddridge (1702–1751), a Nonconformist, who wrote several well-known hymns, including *Ye servants of the Lord* and

WESTON LODGE NEAR OLNEY: WILLIAM COWPER'S RESIDENCE, 1786–1795
Engraving from *Cowper illustrated by a Series of Views*, 1803

Hark! the glad sound, and also *My God, and is Thy table spread,* for a long time the only Communion Hymn at all commonly sung in the Church of England. Augustus Toplady (1740–1778) wrote *Rock of ages,* once well known as Mr. Gladstone's favourite hymn. Not much else of his survives. Dr. Grosart in Julian's *Dictionary of Hymnology* complains that "he has mere vanishing gleams of imaginative light." John Byrom (1692–1763) is known by a single piece but it is a very good one, a Christmas hymn which he wrote for his daughter, *Christians, awake, salute the happy morn,* admirably solid, devotional, and scriptural. He seems to have been an interesting person. *The Dictionary of National Biography* describes him as "poet and

27

stenographer." His poems often did not amount to more than rhymes (at which he was an adept); his shorthand got him made a Fellow of the Royal Society. Some tiny verses of his have found their way into the *English Hymnal* (*My spirit longs for thee*), but they may be too slight to survive.

EIGHTEENTH-CENTURY CHARACTERISTICS

WATTS belongs to the beginning of the eighteenth century, Charles Wesley to the middle, and Cowper to the end of it. Cowper died in 1800 and this may be said to mark the close of the great formative period of English hymn writing. Several different circumstances combined to make it so. The subject-matter, hitherto largely confined to the Psalms, was now extended over the wide field of the whole Bible and into the realm of religious experience, thus offering new and unexploited opportunities. The demand for hymns was intensified by the Methodist movement. The verse was restricted in general to the ballad metre or something similar. The hymns had to be written in the popular language of the day, and at no period has popular language been so simple and graceful or more happily suited to the kind of thing that hymns are.

Of this language perhaps a little more may be said. In the eighteenth century generally speaking the language of verse was elaborate and fanciful and full of classical allusions. Such was the style of Pope and Gray, but then Pope and Gray evidently wrote for the better-educated part of the community. One needed to know a good deal to appreciate them. One needed among other things pagan mythology, and the ordinary hymn singers then had no more use for that than the hymn singers of to-day. But fortunately the typical prose of the eighteenth century on the other hand was plain. Addison wrote his Essays in a plain style. Hume wanted above all things to make his philosophy plain. Law in *The Serious Call* is as plain as a pikestaff. Goldsmith as a prose writer is all ease and plain language. And it was this language to which the hymn writers had recourse. The best prose writers of the period tried very successfully to write much as they spoke, and the hymn writers did the same. In fact they were bound to do so, since they were writing largely for people who read very little besides their hymn books. But this did not mean that they need be dull or low, because they could draw a great deal on the Bible for both incident and language. Charles Wesley does this wonderfully, and although some of the Biblical allusions and echoes must have been lost on many in the congregation, yet some of them must have stuck, and where the words did not remind people of something they knew already, they may have taught them something fresh.

A good example of all this is in Watts's *Cradle Hymn*:

> Yet to read the shameful story
> How the Jews abus'd their King;
> How they served the Lord of Glory
> Makes me angry while I sing.

There are very natural turns of expression here, but it has also an echo of St. Paul in 1 Corinthians ii. 8, "Had they known it they would not have crucified the Lord of glory". In Wesley such Biblical echoes are everywhere. For example:

> Come, Almighty to deliver,
> Let us all Thy grace receive;
> Suddenly return, and never,
> Never more Thy temples leave

where the quiet simple petition alludes both to the prophet's words, "The Lord, whom ye seek shall suddenly come to his temple" (Mal. iii. 1) and to St. Paul's question, "Know ye not that ye are the temple of God?" (1 Cor. iii. 16).

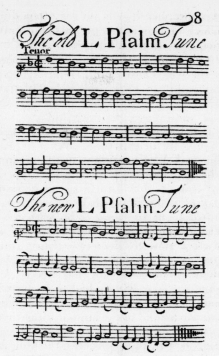

The Lord, the Judge before His Throne
The old and the new tune to Psalm L
From Dr. Watts's *Psalms of David*

And then as to the tunes. The most important fact about them is that they did not differ much from the popular tunes of the day. That is easily perceived by anyone who goes to see and hear *The Beggar's Opera*. John Gay, the author of it, wrote with the express purpose of avoiding the expense of new music and fitted his numbers to tunes already familiar. And when we hear them nowadays we are inclined to say that so many of them are like hymn tunes. It would be truer of course to say that hymn tunes are like the airs in *The Beggar's Opera*. And the quality of these airs we know from a passage in Boswell's *Life of Johnson*. Boswell was an enthusiast for *The Beggar's Opera* because he found in it "so much of real London life, so much brilliant wit, and such a variety of airs, which from early association of ideas engage, soothe, and enliven the mind" (Boswell, under 18 April 1775). Now that is just what is wanted in a hymn, that it should "engage, soothe, and enliven the mind." And it is what the tunes of William Croft and Jeremiah Clark and many other composers of their time well known and little known actually do. The tunes were quickly learned, they were cheerful, and they were easy in performance whether sung in unison or in parts. They were just what John Wesley had in view when he gave his directions to his ministers.

One famous tune has an interesting history from this point of view. It is the well-known tune *Helmsley* which goes to *Lo, He comes with clouds descending*. The Methodist Thomas Olivers is said to have heard a boy whistling it in the street and to have written it down. It is thought that the boy must have been whistling a song by Thomas Carter (d. 1804) then much in vogue. But there was, or rather was to be, another element of popularity in this tune. When it was already famous as a hymn tune the celebrated vocalist Miss Catley (afterwards Mrs. Lascelles) turned it to a different use and danced a hornpipe to it at Vauxhall. There is nothing at all strange of course in popular airs becoming hymn tunes; and in a lesser degree hymn tunes also become popular airs, and would do so more often if it were not for association with religion. Many periods in the Church's history can show instances of secular music being attached to religious words with a view to attracting those who are outside the Church and church-going. In modern times the evangelists Moody and Sankey drew crowds to their missions to sing new words to old tunes, a process very much easier than to persuade people to sing old words to new tunes. People love old tunes, while consciously they hardly care at all about the words, as is shown by the very common practice of singing *Abide with me* at a football match. *Abide with me* makes a very odd introduction (or should I say Introit?) to the game, if you think of it. But the football crowd does not think of it.

The manner of singing a hymn in the eighteenth century must have varied a good deal. One thing is certain. They were never or almost never sung in cathedrals, and they do in fact spoil the perfection of Mattins or Evensong properly rendered in cathedral style. They were often sung at occasional gatherings in the open air or in any sort of room where people could assemble, and later on in church. Even after hymn books were common the old custom called "lining-out" still prevailed in many places. The clerk who was nominally at any rate the musical director read out the first line, and then the people sang it. He then read out the next line and they sang that, and so forth. It sounds tedious, but where the people could not read or had no books, it was the only way, and it served for Psalms and hymns alike. Watts is said to have attended to his versification with "lining-out" in view, that is to say he avoided a line which taken by itself would make nonsense. The words *Jesus lives! no longer now*, for example, would not lend themselves to "lining-out." As time went on, greater skill destroyed the custom, though it died hard; people said it was "the proper way." It was succeeded by the practice of having a band to support the singing, usually in a gallery at the back. In country churches the instruments were of a rustic kind and depended for their effect on the musical talent available

30

THE SERMON
Engraving, 1813, after a painting by Richard Westall

at any particular time. A good musician might take charge and make something of it, but the noise more often than not must have been excruciating.
Thomas Hardy has given a good description of it all in his novel, *Under the
Greenwood Tree*, originally intended to be called *The Mellstock Choir*. In
the preface to the book he has given a lively account of the village choir as
it was about the time of George IV.

31

BY the end of the eighteenth century then the tradition as to the manner and matter of hymns in English was established. In the nineteenth century perhaps the most notable feature is the increase in their number. This is largely due to hymn singing being taken up by High Churchmen, for this meant that the treasury of the ancient Church would be ransacked for what would serve the purpose, and this treasury was very large and very full of treasures.

But before this development could take place it was necessary that hymn singing should get some sort of authorisation in the Church of England. It seems strange now that there should have been any hesitation about this, but so it was. The stiffer people held out for a long time for the Psalms and Gospel Canticles as the only songs of the Church. In 1775 William Romaine maintained this position and asked, "why Dr. Watts or any other hymn writer should take precedence of the Holy Ghost?" Other people who were rather less strict were inclined to confine hymns to such as paraphrased a passage of scripture or at least were plainly based upon it. And experience seems to suggest that if a hymn cannot be headed in the old-fashioned way by a text from Scripture it is not really very suitable for Church use. Be that as it may, the whole idea of hymns as we now know them was for a very long time under suspicion. They seem to have found official recognition only in 1819 when the Rev. Thomas Cotterill, a Sheffield vicar, was brought into the York Diocesan Court for using a hymn book which he and his organist had compiled. The Archbishop, Edward Vernon, afterwards Harcourt (1757–1847), settled the matter and incidentally the principle it involved by requesting the withdrawal of this particular book and sanctioning, and what is more paying for, the publication of a revised edition in the next year.

In the production of this hymnal Cotterill had the assistance of one of our great hymn writers, James Montgomery (1771–1854), a newspaper editor and proprietor, and the author of much poetry, not to be confused with the Robert Montgomery whom Macaulay cut up in one of his essays. James is the writer of the very well known *Hail to the Lord's Anointed, Palms of glory, Songs of praise the angels sang,* and the now slightly obsolescent *For ever with the Lord.* Hardly less familiar are *Angels from the realms of glory, Go to dark Gethsemane* (a Good Friday hymn), and *Lord, teach us how to pray aright.* This is a fine group of carefully written, yet popular hymns.

It is characteristic of the period to which Montgomery belongs that all sorts and conditions of men and women now begin to write hymns, and to publish them either by performance in a church or by contributing them to a journal, which was often rather an obscure one. It is perhaps in the scattered stores of these years (about 1800–1830) that we are most likely now to find pieces that ought to be rescued from oblivion.

INTERIOR OF THE ROYAL CHAPEL, BRIGHTON
Coloured aquatint after W. H. Mason, 1830

To the same period belongs Henry Francis Lyte (1793–1847), who might
in a way claim to be the most celebrated of hymn writers, for he is the
author of *Abide with me,* which has already been mentioned incidentally.
Lyte was the Evangelical incumbent of Lower Brixham, and in 1834 he
produced a volume of hymn-like poems based upon the Psalms, not much
different from many of that time. It contains a really great hymn, *Praise,
my soul, the King of heaven.* But this has been overshadowed by the inten-
sity and the rhetoric of *Abide with me,* of which it may perhaps be fairly
said that it is a very fine specimen of its kind, but the kind is all wrong. Or
at least it seems so now, though it has in its time been a great reality to many.
The tune had much to do with its vogue, composed, so it is said, by W. H.
Monk in ten minutes. Tunes were inclining at that time to the sugary and
mawkish. Part-songs were in fashion, and hymns were affected by the pre-
vailing fashion. They were more suitable for the drawing-room than for
solid straightforward congregational singing. Middle-class families, I have
been told, gathered round the piano and sang hymns on Sunday evenings,
until they dissolved in tears.

33

THE OXFORD MOVEMENT

BUT soon there was to be a great step forward. The Catholic revival in the English Church, commonly called the Oxford Movement, was particularly concerned with giving a new emphasis to worship as it is embodied in the Book of Common Prayer. And for this purpose hymns were required for the Feasts and Fasts of the Church, Office hymns for Morning and Evening Prayer, and more Communion hymns with a rather different tone from those of Wesley and Doddridge. Speaking generally the adherents of the movement thought very much of institutional religion and much less of that "experimental divinity" which the Wesleyan hymn book exhibited. It was natural therefore that they should go back to the hymns of the ancient Church and try to resuscitate them. They resuscitated the Plainsong too which had not been heard in England for three centuries. They made great additions and alterations in the musical parts of the service.

The amount of work they put into this was prodigious, and they soon showed that it was not for nothing that their movement came from Oxford.

CAROL SINGER
Detail from a Christmas card
c. 1876

In many ways it was quite incompatible with Oxford, as Oxford then was and has still remained. But the general culture of the place qualified the Tractarians, as they came to be called, to rout out the proper hymns and translate them successfully from the Latin and sometimes from the Greek. And a great number of these ancient hymns have become part and parcel of English hymnody.

The greatest single contribution was in actual fact made by a Cambridge man, John Mason Neale (1818–1866), son of a Senior Wrangler, himself a very good classic and a man of extraordinary industry and enterprise. He wrote a number of substantial volumes of Church History and many pamphlets besides his hymns, and was the founder of a great convent which is still at East Grinstead, where Neale was Warden of the charming-looking almshouse called Sackville College. He had a wonderfully facility both in translation and in original composition. He did not often try to imitate the metres of the original Latin, so that he was able to keep the ease of English versification, but he also kept

WITH CAROL SWEET AND MERRY LAY
WE GLADLY WELCOME NEW YEAR'S DAY!

CAROL SINGERS
Christmas card, *c.* 1878

something of the feel of the Latin. He translated the very long and elaborate *Hora novissima* of Bernard of Morlaix. *Jerusalem the golden*, and *Brief life is here our portion*, and *For thee, O dear, dear country*, and *The world is very evil* are all parts of this same poem and all frequently sung as hymns. When Neale tried a more elaborate metre in order to translate Abelard's *O quanta qualia* (*Oh what the joy and the glory must be*) he was not quite successful, and in recent times a better translation has been made by Monsignor Ronald Knox, which is in the *Westminster Hymnal*, the book officially compiled for English-speaking Roman Catholics. It would be possible to fill a page with the first lines of well-known hymns by Neale, and his familiarity with a great range of Latin hymns gave strength and force to his original verse. He wrote children's hymns too, among them *Around the throne of God*, and the words of the carol, *Good King Wenceslas.*

He broke new ground when in 1862 he published a volume of translations and adaptations of *Hymns from the Eastern Church.* He spoke of "the immense difficulty of an attempt so new as the present, when I have had no predecessors, and therefore could have no master." A close rendering would not often produce a serviceable hymn in English. But Neale's great sympathy with the Orthodox Greek Church enabled him to catch and

35

convey the spirit of the Greek hymns and shape them for use in English churches without keeping strictly to the text. He has not had many successors in this particular work and very few to rival him. Of the twenty-two hymns listed in the English Hymnal as being 'from the Greek' just half are by Neale, including such favourites as *Stars of the morning, so gloriously bright, The day is past and over,* and the Christmas carol *A great and mighty wonder.*

Second to Neale in translating from the Latin is Edward Caswall, an Oxonian (1814–1878). He became a Roman Catholic and worked in the Birmingham Oratory with Cardinal Newman. He was a more finished verse-maker than Neale. It is interesting to compare their translations of the anonymous *Jesu dulcis memoria.* This is by Neale:

> Jesu, the hope of souls forlorn,
> How good to them for sin that mourn!
> To them that seek thee, oh how kind!
> But what art Thou to them that find?
>
> No tongue of mortal can express,
> No pen can write the blessedness,
> He only who hath proved it knows
> What bliss from love of Jesus flows.

And this is by Caswall:

> O hope of every contrite heart,
>   O Joy of all the meek,
> To those who ask how kind Thou art,
>   How good to those who seek!
>
> But what to those who find? Ah! this
>   Nor tongue nor pen can show;
> The love of Jesus what it is
>   None but his loved ones know.

More graceful than Neale, but just a trifle light-weight. Caswall's *My God, I love Thee* owes most of its excellence perhaps to the beauty of St. Francis Xavier's original.

Neale and Caswall are the leaders in translating hymns to supply what the Oxford Movement needed. In the way of original hymns the greatest names would be those of Cardinal Newman, John Keble, and Frederick Faber, the first two Fellows of Oriel, and the last a Fellow of University College. John Henry Newman (1801–1890) is so famous that he scarcely needs description. He was that rare phenomenon, a man with an equal mastery of words in

36

JOHN HENRY NEWMAN
Chalk drawing by George Richmond, c. 1840

verse and in prose. His controversial writings have not grown stale as such writings usually do. Of his verses *Lead, kindly light,* and *Praise to the Holiest in the height* have been familiar to a vast number of people. The former hardly makes a good hymn, it is too personal, and so far it has not really had a successful tune, but *Praise to the Holiest,* which is from the *Dream of Gerontius* is a most admirable example of a hymn sufficiently poetical, suitable for congregational use, and at the same time thoroughly doctrinal and devotional. *Firmly I believe and truly* makes a good High Church hymn.

John Keble (1792–1866) was gifted in a different way. He is less accomplished, not often brilliant, but always sound. His *Christian Year* must have been one of the most widely diffused books of religious verse in the world. But it is intended primarily for devotional reading and is not a hymn book. Nevertheless it has had an important influence, because it has given a great many people their idea of the tone they look for in a hymn. About a dozen pieces from the *Christian Year* are suitable for congregational singing in church, and two or three are very good for the purpose. *Blest are the pure in heart,* part of the poem for the Feast of the Purification, is as well known

37

as any, and *There is a book, who runs may read* ranks high as the exposition of the truth that God is visible in Nature. Keble's influence as a devout parish priest and a poet extended very far.

And thirdly, there is Frederick Faber (1814–1863), who like Newman and Caswall was an Oratorian. He is very interesting, because he is so sentimental. Occasionally this gets the better of him as in *Hark, hark, my soul*, which is really about *nothing*, but when he keeps his talent in control he shows what a place there is for sentimental hymns, and what they can be. *My God, how wonderful Thou art* is such a hymn and so is the one which is sometimes made to begin with *There's a wideness in God's mercy* and sometimes with *Souls of men! why will ye scatter*. This is a great converting and teaching hymn.

23

HYMN V.

As the mother stilleth every little noise.

THE glorious sun is set in the west; the night dews fall; and the air, which was sultry, becomes cool.

The flowers fold up their

WOODCUT FROM MRS. BARBAULD'S *HYMNS FOR CHILDREN*

There is plentiful redemption
    In the Blood that has been shed;
There is joy for all the members
    In the sorrows of the Head.

For the love of God is broader
    Than the measure of man's mind;
And the Heart of the Eternal
    Is most wonderfully kind.

The taste for ancient hymns which the Tractarians successfully fostered was accompanied by a taste for ancient melodies to sing them to. But the acceptance of Plainsong Chant and Melody has not been nearly so wide as the acceptance of the words. This is partly due to the advocates of Plainsong being too rigid and pure. What the public was offered required a great deal of getting used to, and generally speaking English hymn singers never have got used to it. At the same time with suitable modifications the *Manual of Plainsong* associated mainly with the name of Thomas Helmore (1811–1890) and the *Hymnal Noted* in which Neale collaborated with Benjamin Webb (1819–1885) have had a great influence on our Church music.

WOMEN HYMN WRITERS

THE full range of English Hymnody may well be said to have been completed in the second quarter of the nineteenth century, and it is noteworthy that then or thereabouts women began to make a great contribution to our stock of hymns. The first to be named amongst them ought surely to be Cecil Frances Alexander (1818–1895), wife of a well-known Archbishop of Armagh. She had a gift all her own for writing children's hymns which were scriptural and graceful and, if particularly suitable for children, yet also much liked by grown-ups too. *Once in Royal David's City, All things bright and beautiful, We are but little children weak* all have a peculiar charm. She did not confine herself to the children; *Jesus calls us o'er the tumult* and *His are the thousand sparkling rills* are good examples of what she could do. As to the very familiar *There is a green hill far away* it is hard to know if it is a children's hymn or not. It is very simple, but then it is very profound, for it deals in quite a masterly way with several aspects of the Atonement.

WOODCUT
FROM CATHERINE WINKWORTH'S
LYRA GERMANICA

Two other women, Frances Cox (1812–1897) and Catherine Winkworth (1827–1878), both did a special work in putting German hymns into an English dress. Miss Winkworth is the better known and has had the greater influence through her *Lyra Germanica* (1855), but the best work of Miss Cox is admirable. They have both translated the famous *Wachet auf* (*Sleepers, wake*) and their respective versions are worth comparing. The heart-stirring *Now thank we all our God* is by Miss Winkworth.

HYMNS ANCIENT AND MODERN

IT is easy to guess that in the course of all this activity a great variety of hymn books would become available, and congregations would always be discovering hymns they wanted to use which were not in their particular collection. And soon it was bound to occur to someone to try and consolidate the most serviceable hymns in a new book. This was done very successfully in *Hymns Ancient and Modern*. The first suggestion is said to have come from the Rev. F. H. Murray, Rector of Chislehurst, in 1857. It was taken up by others, amongst whom was Sir H. W. Baker, himself a prolific hymn writer, the author of *The King of Love my shepherd is*, and after Neale the largest single contributor to *Ancient and Modern*. The proprietors of other hymn books agreed to collaborate, and the book was launched in 1861. It contained 273 hymns. Seven years later this was raised to 386. In 1875 the book was thoroughly revised and contained 473 hymns. A Supplement was added in 1889, bringing the total to 638. Its success was tremendous, and quite surprised the proprietors, partly because, like Wesley before them, they found it made them so rich.

It is natural to ask the reason for this success, and the answer probably lies mainly in the music. Desirable or not, the fact remains that when people say they like a hymn they generally mean that they like the tune. And it must be allowed that the tunes provided in the book were mostly very like-able. Few of them were florid or difficult, and many of them easily caught the ear. Of course some very bad tunes fulfilled these conditions, but so also do some of the best tunes in the world. Much of the music has been superseded, especially what the Rev. J. B. Dykes contributed, yet nothing did more to popularise the book than Dr. Dykes's tunes, and some of his will probably prove indispensable for a very long time to come. His tune for *Jesu, Lover of my soul* has already been widely displaced by the tune *Aberystwyth*, his tune for *Eternal Father, strong to save* enjoys an un-diminished vogue.

So much for the tunes. But the words, though much less important from the point of view of immediate circulation, could make or mar a hymn book in the long run. It takes much longer for the words to become endeared to the people, and a very long time before they see that these or those bad words really will not do. But they do come to it in the end. And here the compilers of *Hymns Ancient and Modern* did wonderfully well. They took Keble's hint to be comprehensive, though it is true that in their earlier editions they neglected the eighteenth century rather unduly. The hymns were pretty literally Ancient and Modern. The best of the ancient hymns were there in one form or another. The bulk of the remainder were by living authors or those not long departed. But the success of the book is not to be accounted for quite so simply. The striking thing about it is its unified tone. It looks as if some one person must have had a very correct feeling as to what was in keeping with the book and what was not. We cannot fail to admire the great tact with which sobriety and emotion are made to go hand in hand. Here it looks as if some single mind was at work. But whose?

Another feature of the book is the sensible way in which the compilers altered the text where it contained what for some reason or other was inad-missible for congregational singing. With the modern taste for research a notion arose towards the end of last century that there was some peculiar merit in the original version of a hymn as the author wrote it. There certainly

A MID-VICTORIAN CONGREGATION
Coloured print from *Hymns and Pictures*, London, 1860

A SERVICE IN ST. PAUL'S CATHEDRAL
Baxter print by Bradshaw and Blacklock, c. 1872
By courtesy of the Librarian of the Guildhall Library

might be if a hymn book was a manual of English literature, but it is not. And a good deal of pedantry has crept into recent hymn books. The proprietors of *Hymns Ancient and Modern* were guilty of it themselves to their cost when they went back in their new edition of 1904 to Charles Wesley's *Hark how all the welkin rings* for which *Hark! the herald angels sing* had become a universal alternative. One other example of the same sort of thing must suffice. The *Hymns Ancient and Modern* omitted from Cowper's splendid *God moves in a mysterious way* one stanza, namely:

> His purposes will ripen fast
> Unfolding every hour:
> The bud may have a bitter taste,
> But sweet will be the flower.

Surely a wise omission, for who knows from experience which buds have a bitter taste, and who eats flowers? Yet misplaced learning has bid the stanza creep back again in some books in order to have the whole hymn as Cowper wrote it. All things considered, the *Hymns Ancient and Modern* was a very judicious work. In the nineteenth century only one book perhaps may be said to have rivalled it. This was called *Church Hymns* and was evolved by the Society for Promoting Christian Knowledge from a book of *Hymns and Psalms* which the Society had published in 1855. It came out in 1870, and for some years was very popular, largely owing to the musical editorship of Sir Arthur Sullivan. But a new edition published rather more than thirty years later failed to catch on, though it is a good book. Mention may also be made here of a book in no wise to be overlooked, the *Church Hymnary,* which is the official hymn book of the Church of Scotland, a collection which has been re-edited from time to time and seems now almost adequate to what is best and most characteristic in Presbyterianism. It is based on a sure foundation, namely a tradition some centuries old of Psalm singing in the Metrical version.

DISSATISFACTION

IT looked as though English Christianity had now got the hymns it wanted. But in matters of this sort there is no standing still. Already, as we have seen, there had been a long slow development. The Metrical Psalms had been amplified with the scriptural and evangelical hymns of the eighteenth century, and these again by the hymns from ancient sources which hardly anyone but Bishop Cosin of Durham had delved into before the Oxford Movement. The taste and tone of mid-Victorianism had absorbed all this and was still supplementing what it had got with more of its own invention. The *Hymns Ancient and Modern* had few effective rivals, and at first its critics were to be found only among those whose views were somewhat extreme. The Evangelicals had the *Hymnal Companion* (1870) from which its editors excluded what seemed to be too "High Church." Those who on the other hand wanted more hymns from the Latin found them in the *Hymnary* (not to be confused with the *Church Hymnary* just mentioned above). This is a work of trained discrimination, but rather inappropriately beautified with a number of tunes by Sir Joseph Barnby, intended perhaps to moderate the severity of the words.

In general the tendency after 1860 was towards verse that was overornamental and tunes that were sweet. The fact that church-going was fashionable did little good to hymn singing. The particular piety of the time, which was both prosperous and public-spirited, contrived to put up large organs in almost every church, often much too large an organ. The choir and band in the gallery had been liquidated, and a surpliced choir, sometimes more numerous than musical, had appeared in the chancel. The cathedral type of service had become the ideal for the ordinary parish church, and *The Cathedral Prayer Book* was in the parson's stall. In this book every service is choral, even the service for the Churching of Women. But in all this there was the inherent contradiction that Cathedral Service offers very little scope for hymns; indeed they tend to spoil it. Yet hymns had come to be taken for granted in parish churches. So the choir wanted to sing them in elaborate parts, and the congregation grew in some degree content to let the choir do the singing for them. Consequently we have witnessed a decline in singing in the last fifty or sixty years, resulting in a latent dissatisfaction which has so far been only partly remedied by new ideas in hymnody. Notable among those ideas has been the introduction of folksong tunes and unison hymns which in the old *Hymns Ancient and Modern* went almost wholly unrepresented.

ROBERT BRIDGES

THIS dissatisfaction which came to a head at the end of the nineteenth century found its most methodical and really most important exponent in Robert Bridges, the late Poet Laureate (1844–1930). His *Yattendon Hymnal* and the short essays which he wrote in connection with it deserve careful study, not only as the work of a skilled musician and an eminent literary man, but because he laid his finger precisely on the sore even if he did not altogether heal it. His characterisations of the most notable stages in the practice of hymn-singing are very good. He praises the Plainsong melodies: "Sing to anyone a plainsong melody, *Ad coenam Agni* for instance, once or twice, and then Croft's 148th Psalm. Croft will be undeniably fine and impressive, but he provokes a smile: his tune is like

WOODCUT FROM DR. WATTS'S *DIVINE AND MORAL SONGS FOR CHILDREN*
Edition of 1866

a diagram beside a flower." Bourgeois's tunes, he says, "in dignity, solemnity, pathos, and melodic solidity leave nothing to be desired." Of the chorale style which prevailed at the end of the sixteenth century he says that "the broad, sonorous swell of its harmonious intervals floods the air with peaceful power." Then after praising "Jeremy Clark, Croft, and others" he speaks of a degradation of style. "These weak ditties, in the admired manner of Lord Mornington, were typically performed by the genteel pupils of the local musician, who, gathered round him beneath the laughing cherubs of the organ case, warbled by abundant candle-light to their respectful audience with a graceful execution that rivalled the weekday performance of *Celia's Arbour* and the *Spotted Snakes*." This brings him to "modern church music" which "has for one chief differentiation the profuse employment of pathetic chords, the effect of which is often disastrous to the feelings." These opinions Bridges expressed in 1899 in his *Practical Discourse on some Principles of Hymn Singing*, now *XXII* of his *Collected Essays*. And with such notions in his head he proceeded to make his collection of one hundred hymns. It is remarkable among hymn books for the fewness of the hymns, but all of them are good, and it is difficult to imagine it destined to be so much the sport of fashion as most hymn books. Furthermore to fit the tunes he wanted, Bridges himself wrote or adapted the words of 44 out of his 100 items. Amongst them are many admirable pieces, correct and solid, heartfelt yet not too arresting, and admirably suited to be sung to these tunes, none of which in fact was composed later than about 1720. The very short piece headed *In time of war* (No. 54) is a model of what a hymn should be:

> Rejoice, O land, in God thy might.
> His will obey, Him serve aright.
> For thee the saints uplift their voice.
> Fear not, O land, in God rejoice.
>
> Glad shalt thou be, with blessing crown'd.
> With joy and peace thou shalt abound.
> Yea, love with thee shall make his home,
> Until thou see God's kingdom come.
>
> He shall forgive thy sins untold.
> Remember thou His love of old.
> Walk in His way, His word adore,
> And keep His truth for evermore.

The *Yattendon Hymnal* cannot be said to have been exactly a success. There are not enough hymns, there are hardly any institutional hymns, because to Bridges anything churchy, and one might say anything theological too, was deeply suspect; there is more medieval music than people care for. And the book in its first edition cost a pound and could not be easily got. Bridges showed a singular gift for preventing the circulation of all his works except *The Testament of Beauty*. Nevertheless his influence has been very great. He has revived Bourgeois. He has stopped the ornamental style. He has persuaded many that the tunes matter a lot. He has shown above all that hymns can be manly. *The Oxford Hymn Book* was compiled largely on his principles. It extends the number of hymns to 350 and makes some provision for the Church's seasons, though not enough for practical purposes. It contains extremely beautiful things, but it has not taken on as a parish-church book owing to its limited range.

RECENT HYMN BOOKS

THE *English Hymnal* owes much to Bridges too. It has had a great and deserved success, since it tapped many sources and had the hardihood to throw out a good deal that was popular and bad. Its tendency is towards the "High Church" presentation of things, yet it is catholic rather than Anglo-Catholic. Some of the pieces composed specially for it already begin to seem rather trifling. But it is a great work and has provided some hymns that are now indispensable, as for example, Athelstan Riley's *Ye watchers and ye holy ones*.

CHOIR BOYS PRACTISING
Chalk drawing by Robert Austin, 1946

The *English Hymnal* appeared in 1906. Two years before, after a great deal of labour, the proprietors of *Hymns Ancient and Modern* had produced an entirely new edition of their book. It was a remarkably good book, but it was a failure. Possibly it was in advance of its time; at any rate people would not be persuaded to take it up. The proprietors were obliged to go back to the old book and reprint it with a second supplement (1916), which made it too bulky, though usefully comprehensive.

Hymns Ancient and Modern and *The English Hymnal* are definitely Church of England Books, though any denomination would find most of what it wants in them. But it seemed to some that in the modern world there was room for a hymn book which might be used in church but also beyond the confines of a church, at interdenominational meetings or in connection with social activities that were almost detached from any ecclesiastical organisation. The *Songs of Praise* was designed to meet this demand. It contains a great deal of both old and new material, some of which stands quite apart from the historical tradition. Doctrinal assertion is avoided where it can be, and some famous hymns have been watered down for this purpose. Perhaps the positive idea that underlies the book is to be found in its title. Hymns should be songs, and songs they often are in the *Songs of Praise*. In consequence a fresh kind of pleasure has been found in hymns and a new sense of fellowship in congregational singing. The work also makes a nice poetry book. But it is possible that it exploits too much what is only a passing phase. It also has its eye on youth, and on schools and colleges; a lot of it is not quite grown-up, and in the end that can no more please the young than the old.

HYMNS FROM AMERICA

ENGLISH hymns have naturally spread over the British Empire, and there has also of course been a free interchange of hymns between this country and the United States. The extent of it is worth a brief reckoning. The earlier settlers took the Metrical Psalter with them. The very first hymn book out of the many which Wesley produced was actually printed in Charlestown (now a part of Boston) in 1737, and was described on the title page as by John Wesley, Missioner of Georgia. A passage of hymns in the opposite direction, from America to England, resulted from the tours in this country between 1870 and 1880 of Dwight L. Moody (1837–1899) and Ira D. Sankey (1840–1908), a pair of American evangelists. Moody's preaching and Sankey's singing combined towards the conversion of tens of thousands. Sankey collected the music they used into a book called *Sacred Songs and Solos*. They became famous, even notorious, for their indifference to traditional styles both in words and music. Many of the pieces were popular songs of the crudest kind with many repetitions and choruses. But Sankey possessed in a very high degree the art of managing community singing. The tunes caught on because they were catchy, and the words repeated and emphasised the simplest gospel appeal. They were not valuable as poetry or music, but they were well adapted to their purpose. It is usual to say that they were inspired by the camp-fire sing-songs of the backwoods, which in a way only amounts to saying that they were folk-songs. They kept down to the level of the gatherings for which they were intended, not such a very easy thing to do. The problem nowadays is to perform the same service for a crowd at a somewhat higher level of education, particularly in music.

Whether it was that Sankey's *Sacred Songs and Solos* aroused an interest in American hymns in general or not, certainly in rather more recent times a good many hymns of very superior merit have found their way from America into English hymn books, and particularly into the *English Hymnal*. The chief names are those of the eminent James Russell Lowell (1819–1891), author of *Once to every man and nation*, and the poet John Greenleaf Whittier (1807–1892), who has four pieces in the *English Hymnal*, increased to nine in *Songs of Praise*. The great Oliver Wendell Holmes (1809–1894) is represented in both books by *Lord of all being, throned afar*. *Songs of Praise* which goes far beyond the limits of what may legitimately be called a hymn has Walt Whitman's *Pioneers* and Julia Ward Howe's *Battle Hymn of the Republic* intended for the tune of *John Brown's Body*. To these names may be added those of three American Bishops of note, G. W. Doane (1799–1859), author of *Fling out the banner*; A. C. Coxe (1818–1896), Bishop of Western New York; and the admirable pastor and preacher Phillips Brooks (1835–1893), the author of the carol-like hymn *O little town of Bethlehem*. And no doubt there is much more to come.

Some of these American hymns have a tone of their own. They are decidedly ethical and give expression to Theism or even Deism rather than to anything specifically Christian. They tend a little to sermonise. Lowell does not speak for himself alone when he says: "I shall never be a poet till I get out of the pulpit."

CONCLUSION

IT is sometimes said that for the Church of England or even possibly for English-speaking Christianity as a whole there ought to be an official hymn book put forth and approved by authority. But that would have the effect of freezing what is as yet a lively, flowing stream. The compilers of a hymn book, like a good steward, take out of their store things old and new. There is still undoubtedly a harvest to be gathered from the past, and on the other hand new hymns and hymn tunes are still being written and launched successfully on the hymn-singing public. Of this fresh material, as always in such cases, much will fall back into disuse, but something is always being added to the permanent stock. It may be that a canon of hymns will gradually form itself. For if works of art are constantly impressed upon the public, the public eventually knows what will do and what will not. We need poets and composers and critics to turn our attention in the right direction, but it is the great company of hymn-singing Christians who will decide finally what is to be in the books and what is not, and in the end all the books will probably turn out to have much the same collection in use. The canon will have been formed. And it must be noted that the process is only made possible by the happy practice which has always existed (as indeed it should) of allowing the compilers of hymn books to borrow freely from one another on the payment of some nominal fee. If any other point of view had prevailed, the *Ancient and Modern* could never have come into existence, nor any of the great comprehensive hymn books. And upon the continuance of this view depends ultimately the expression of the common mind of those who sing hymns in the English tongue.

But are hymns really works of art then? The answer is "Yes" decidedly. But although they use the same material as the art of poetry, hymns are not poetry except by coincidence, and to say that a hymn is good or bad poetry is not to settle the question whether it is a good or bad hymn. For so much depends on the tune, and so little on the superior excellence of the verse. The fancies in the sense and the subtle variations in the metre which go so much to make good poetry are nothing but hindrances in a hymn. The words should fit the tune, and while they are being sung there is no time to stop and admire the fancy. Plain words, plain metre, plain sense are the first requirements. They may be solemn or they may be gay, but they must be religious and they had best be scriptural. They must do something to elevate and instruct the singer. It is not so easy to work within this limited field, but at happy moments it has been beautifully done. Hymn writing perhaps bears something of the same relation to poetry that illumination does to easel painting.

At any rate in Britain it is one of the national arts and one of the national institutions.